THE PRIDE OF
DRAGONS
ORACLE

T0405433

THE PRIDE OF

DRAGONS
ORACLE

A 44-CARD DECK AND GUIDEBOOK

A Sacred Planet Deck

ANGELO THOMAS
ARTWORK BY SONJA HEDGER

Bear & Company
Rochester, Vermont

Bear & Company
One Park Street
Rochester, Vermont 05767
www.BearandCompanyBooks.com

Bear & Company is a division of Inner Traditions International

Sacred Planet Books are curated by Richard Grossinger, Inner Traditions editorial board member and cofounder and former publisher of North Atlantic Books. The Sacred Planet collection, published under the umbrella of the Inner Traditions family of imprints, includes works on the themes of consciousness, cosmology, alternative medicine, dreams, climate, permaculture, alchemy, shamanic studies, oracles, astrology, crystals, hyperobjects, locutions, and subtle bodies.

ISBN 978-1-59143-492-4 (print)

Printed and bound in China by Reliance Printing Co., Ltd.

10 9 8 7 6 5 4 3 2 1

Text design and layout by Virginia Scott Bowman
This book was typeset in Garamond Premier Pro with Majesty used as the display typeface

To send correspondence to the author of this book, mail a first-class letter to the author c/o Inner Traditions • Bear & Company, One Park Street, Rochester, VT 05767, and we will forward the communication, or contact the author directly at **www.AngeloThomas.com.au**.

✧

The dragons' love for humanity is unbreakable

Their power is immeasurable and their feats for humans match the most angelic of natures

The day all humans realize they can call upon the dragons to assist them on the journey to their highest good is what we are all working toward in the angelic realms

Take time today to notice one of the many dragons around you, for they will show themselves

Simply ask them gently to step forward and they will.

ARCHANGEL GABRIEL,
CHANNELED BY THE AUTHOR

Contents

THE DRAGONS

The Pride of the Fallen

The Pride of the Earthly

The Pride of the Heavenly

The Pride of the Archangels

Working with Dragons

Dragons have been depicted by more cultures throughout human history than any other mystical beast, even more so than unicorns or phoenixes.

Of all the angelic beings, the dragons are the only ones to have spiritual bodies made of earthly elemental energies, as we do. Like the angels, however, they have no divine free will, and must always be of service to humanity, so long as their intervention is for our highest good. Due to this dual nature of dragons, they were chosen at this time to be the deliverers of the celestial wisdom.

The dragons have always worked in this style of harmony with the angels to serve humankind, and it is said they created the Earth for us, as well as the crystals we use today.

The dragons also specialize in removing

obstacles in our path that are preventing us from reaching our highest good. They lift our frequency by clearing lower vibrational thought patterns, and fiercely protect us against negative energies. They also gift us with celestial wisdom from the angelic realms.

Dwelling on Earth from within the astral plane, and beyond to the heavens and cosmos above, there are countless dragons we can call upon in our everyday life. And no, not all breathe fire or are winged, serpent-like beasts, as you will discover while working with this oracle deck.

So if you're ready to work with these mystical beasts and access the celestial wisdom they hold, take a journey with the Pride of Dragons and meet your new spirit guides from the angelic realms!

Acknowledgments

To Country

We acknowledge the traditional owners of country throughout Australia, and their continuing connection to land, sea, and community. This deck was created across the traditional lands of the Turrbal and Jagera people, the Larrakia people, and the Kungarakany people. We pay our respects to them, their culture, and their elders both past and present.

To Spirit

We would also like to thank Spirit, for The Call and for our ability to hear it.

We thank each other, for connection and the ability to share it.

We thank you all, for seeking and discovering Spirit.

Grateful and thankful, as collectively we answer The Call.

INTRODUCTION
The Pride of Dragons

The Pride of Dragons is an oracle deck on celestial wisdom as presented by forty-four unique and individual dragons from the angelic realms.

The dragons who stepped forward for this deck are unique in both nature and appearance. Each dragon has its own looks, personality, energy, and even frequency, which determines its color, element, and where it resides in each of the angelic realms. Like angels, dragons do not age or have gender and always present themselves in a youthful appearance and refer to themselves in the third person. Their messages reflect them as individuals—their qualities and the roles they play in service to humanity, on behalf of the angelic realms.

1

In linking to the angelic realms, each dragon works with a specific angel or archangel. Like the dragons, these angels have a specific role and their presence provides further context for and explanation of that dragon's energy, message, and perspective on celestial wisdom.

Each dragon also has its own elemental energies, sometimes one or a combination of many of the five elements (earth, fire, wind, water, and ether). These elements are provided to assist you with finding a tangible tool when connecting with each dragon's energy, which can be symbolic or literal in nature. Examples are a feather, a candle, a crystal, a vessel of water, or even a place in nature to sit and spend time while working with this deck. There is an exception to this—the Archangel Dragons. Their vibration and frequency transcend elemental energies and as such are not aligned to any element(s).

To present their perspective on celestial wisdom, the dragons organized themselves into four prides.

The Pride of the Fallen

This pride gives us wisdom and warnings that are brought forward by four dragons from the realms of the fallen angels. Do not fear these messages, as there is much learning from the fallen. Their wisdom can assist us greatly in our spiritual and personal growth.

The Pride of the Earthly

This pride offers practical wisdom and teachings that are brought forward by fourteen dragons from the realms of earthly angels. These messages relate directly to daily life and are more grounded in nature to reflect the world around us and how we interact with others on this Earth.

The Pride of the Heavenly

This pride brings us wisdom and messages that are presented by fourteen dragons from the realms of the heavenly angels. These messages are aspirational and almost ethereal in nature and, as is the case with heavenly wisdom, they are relevant to any given moment of our lives.

The Pride of the Archangels

Universal celestial messages are brought forward by twelve of the most powerful dragons of the archangel realm. These powerful and direct messages from the archangels are provided for deep, self-introspective thought and reflection. Let these divine messages wash over you initially, then sit and let them unfold over time, for they will constantly take on new meaning and depth.

✦

Although the dragons present themselves in prides, the purpose of this deck is self-development and discovery. You may wish to work with one dragon at a time to truly immerse yourself in its unique energy and wisdom and explore its respective angel and element to further understand the message of the dragon. We'll look at specific ways to work with the dragons of the oracle cards in the following chapter.

The Pendragon

The dragon on the back of each card is known as the Pendragon, which literally means "Chief Dragon" or "Head of the Dragons." The Pendragon does not belong to any pride and instead sits above all the dragons in the deck.

The Pendragon is the embodiment of all dragon energies and its presence brings to the surface an ancient energy connecting us to something tangible from the days of Creation. This is a bringing of light and service to humanity so that we may reconnect with celestial energy and the knowledge that is needed and relied on in current times.

As a result of what is physically occurring on our Earth, and its placement in the universe today, the Pendragon implores us to not ignore the redefining of the ascension process occurring energetically in the background. This shift is enlightening our perspective on spirituality, making way for the coming forth of the celestials in a new light. This includes a newfound acceptance that dragons have always been spiritual beings who have played a diverse role in our ascension process since the birth of Creation.

With this moving away from myth, legend, and stories of magic, the Pendragon commands the dragons to deliver messages, information, and instructions on how to bring forward ancient celestial wisdom and apply this knowledge to everyday life. This in turn delivers a more intimate connection to an otherwise previously inaccessible realm of knowledge.

How to Use This Oracle

In your quest for self-development and discovery, work with an open mind, heart, and soul when approaching the dragons for guidance. In fact, it is important to work from this space when utilizing any form of intuitive practice. Do not be attached to outcomes but rather release and trust.

Quan Yin Blessing

Prior to working with the Pride of Dragons, you may wish to bless your deck in a sacred space of your choosing, one where you won't be disturbed by others. This can be anywhere you feel safe and comfortable. In this blessing we will be using various objects that symbolize each of the four elements (water, fire, air, and earth). (Should you wish to symbolize the fifth element of ether, you can also add a dragon-related crystal such as septarian or dragon's blood jasper to the middle of the circle.) Select and place these objects in a circle and set a single white candle in the middle.

Once the circle is complete, light the candle then take a few drops of frankincense essential oil and rub it between your hands. This oil is known to have a very high vibration and can assist in raising your frequency to that of the dragons.

Next, light the candle, take the cards in your hands and, while shuffling them, recite the following blessing by the ascended master Quan Yin, known by some as the Goddess of the Dragons.

> *Beautiful children of Quan Yin, descend*
> *from the Divine,*
> *You, the angel's kin, please bless me within*
> *Your time for slumber is over, for now is a*
> *new day in the Divine,*
> *I open my heart to you, children of the sky*
> *Descend from the heavens and bathe me*
> *in the Divine,*
> *I open my heart to the dragons*
> *My new celestial guides in the Divine.*

Once you have finished the blessing, place the deck in front of you and sit still while focusing on the flame of the candle in front of you. Watch it dance, watch it play. This is your connection to the angelic breath of the dragons today.

Stay in this moment for as long as you need, and enjoy your sacred time with the dragons.

After some time, you may notice the presence of dragons around you. However, do not worry if you do *not* feel their presence. Simply trust that your intention and prayer has called them in, and they will do the rest.

Now you are ready to work with your Pride of Dragons and begin your new journey into the angelic realms.

Dragon Card Selection

The following methods of selecting and working with the oracle cards will get you started on your journey with the dragons and their celestial wisdom. As you grow more familiar with the Pride of Dragons, you may wish to create your own card selection rituals and spreads in line with your individual practice.

The Sole Dragon

If you have a specific question, or are simply after daily guidance from the dragons, you can pull one card from the deck as required.

When doing so, take a moment to close your eyes and be very clear on your question; try to avoid yes or no questions and focus instead on what you need to learn from a situation or simply be open to whatever it is that the dragons wish for you to know in the here and now.

You can shuffle the cards and, when finished, either choose the one on top or lay them out in front of you facedown and choose one at random. There is no wrong or right way to pull a card, and you can be as creative as you wish.

Once you have pulled a card, sit with the image of the dragon, read the corresponding message in this guidebook, and reflect on all your thoughts in that moment. Also take note of the dragon's corresponding angel and element(s) and consider ways that you might work with these energies. Take in all that this dragon has to offer. Reflect and take as much time as you need.

It might even prove useful to journal each time you do this exercise. You can reflect on your written words later, as well as note your progress in working with the dragons.

The Dragon Guide

Should you wish to call in a dragon and work with its energy over a certain amount of time, simply sit with the deck and invite one to step forward.

Light a candle in a space where you will not be disturbed, and close your eyes.

Shuffle the deck as you call out for a dragon to appear. This can be done silently in your mind or out loud.

When ready, spread the cards in front of you, fanning them out facedown.

In your mind's eye, reach out for the first card that captures your attention and turn it over.

Take this card in your hand and meet your new dragon friend.

Who is this dragon? What is its message? Who is its angel and what is its element?

Take note of its color, face, and unique look—does it resemble a traditional dragon or a more unique, mystical beast?

Get to know this dragon and welcome it in as it takes on the role of your new dragon guide.

It's up to you as to how you now work with this dragon, but know this: respect it and its energy, thank it daily for its presence, and only ever call upon it to assist you when it aligns with the highest good for yourself and others.

A Pride Full

It is also possible to work with multiple dragons at the same time in an oracle card spread. This four-card spread uses all the prides of the deck to receive a message for you and the collective. The collective can be your family, friends, colleagues, or broader community.

To begin, hold the deck in your hands, close your eyes, and take three deep breaths.

Next, open your eyes and sort the cards into four piles according to each pride, starting with the Fallen through the Archangels, from left to right. There's no need for the piles to be tidy, just place them far enough away from each other that they don't mix.

Once you are finished, close your eyes again and ask the dragons for a message for you and your collective.

Using your mind's eye (and your physical eyes, if needed!), reach out and choose a card from each pile (each pride). As you go, lay each card out in front of you from left to right, again following the order of the Fallen to Archangel Pride.

Pride of the Fallen	Pride of the Earthly	Pride of the Heavenly	Pride of the Archangels

Open your eyes and take a moment to reflect on the four dragons in front of you. Who are the four dragons? What are their messages? Who are their angels, and what are their elements?

Take some time to journal your thoughts. As you reflect on these dragons, note what the message is for you and your community. Use these reflections to guide you forward, in a clear and focused manner.

The dragons ask that you read their energy from left to right according to the prides, as you are being taken on a journey. Starting off with wisdom from the dark inner realms, you are then provided with a grounded approach to the upcoming universal message, which will finally be anchored in the light by Source energy. This reflects how the dragons wish for us to undertake any form of spiritual work for the collective. Work on yourself first, take a grounded approach, and call in the light to anchor your actions.

Once you are finished, gather up your cards,

thank the four dragons, and trust that they will be with you going forward.

The Dragon Altar

Did you know you can use your Pride of Dragons deck to create a Dragon Altar?

A Dragon Altar is a space in your home that's dedicated solely to the dragons, which invites them into your life and sets the intention that you wish to work with them daily. Dragon Altars act as a visual acknowledgment of the dragons and are a subtle, everyday reminder of their presence in our lives.

Your Dragon Altar does not have to be big or elaborate, as the very act of having this space sets the intention that you want dragons in your life. It can be a small corner of your living room, on a hallstand in the entrance of your home, or a whole room dedicated to dragons; it's up to you!

Once you have decided on a space for your altar, get started by pulling a card from the deck. Remember, there is no right or wrong way to pull a card.

Place the selected card in the center of your altar and surround it with items that represent the dragon, as well as dragons more broadly, such as

❖ Colored candles that match the color of the dragon or represent its element(s)
❖ Crystals related to dragons, its angel, or its element(s)
❖ Incense to represent the breath of the dragons
❖ Statues, sculptures, or drawings of dragons
❖ Any other object that you are drawn to place in this space that reminds you of dragons

You can choose to keep the same dragon on this altar for however long you wish, or invite a new dragon to take its place when you feel it's necessary.

A Dragon Altar can also be set up when you are traveling, in your hotel room or wherever you're staying, to welcome in the protection, guidance, and healing energies of dragons when you are away from home.

THE DRAGONS

The Pride of

THE FALLEN

1
Serpent of Death

.... ◆ ....

Angel: Azrael, Angel of Death, works to
    force the hand of death
Element: Water assists with the flow of
    the inevitable

A flash of blue followed by a large, black, serpent-like dragon appears underfoot. It moves with elegance and grace for such a devilish beast; one could be forgiven for mistaking it for the biblically referenced Leviathan. However, do not fear this dragon, as it comes for those of us who are long overdue for change and do not realize their stagnation.

When this dragon appears, take a breath, and ask yourself:

What in my life needs to die?
What changes are needed right here and now?

Do this immediately, swiftly, and without hesitation.

Death is change; a transition from one state to another. The same applies here, and like death, you have no choice but to face this change and work with this dragon. Its energy is not to be taken lightly, nor is its message. Do not be afraid of this dragon for it can become one of your greatest allies and will work tirelessly to uncover any answers you seek during this time of change.

All you need to do is simply get out of your own way and allow this Serpent of Death to take the lead and do what it does best—obliterate stagnation and swiftly guide you through this transitional phase.

2
Mirror Realm

·········· ❧ ··········

Angel: Bezaliel, Angel of the Shadows,
   drives the shadows to the surface
Element: Water assists with deep
   inner reflection

Three voices, six eyes, one dragon from the
Mirror Realm. A three-headed dragon of a
fallen angel, this dragon is cursed to live upside
down in our service. As we walk the surface of
this Earth, it walks in the mirrored reflection of
the shadows, a place where nothing is as it seems.
However, *one* thing is certain—as above so below,
as within so without.

When this dragon appears, be still and listen
to its voice, for it speaks in whispered rhymes.

You are being advised to see your situation
from many angles, even in reverse! In the Mirror
Realm nothing can hide—all is seen—and this

dragon's three heads provide it with the perfect advantage!

Are you being deceived, blinded, or even challenged by someone in the shadows?

Pause and reflect: the presence of this dragon is a warning. Much can be learned from wisdom born in the Mirror Realm.

Take time to assess your energy, your space, for lower vibrational thinking and feelings about the treatment of yourself and others—for everything is a reflection of what is within.

3
Rite Poison

.... ◆ ....

Angel: Harut, Angel of Sorcery, helps
   concoct the medicine and deliver
   the correct dose
Element: Water assists with deep
   cleansing

Drums beat in the distance, the rattle of a snake draws near. A fire burns, a sorcerer dances his dance, a red and blue smoke fills the land. A dragon steps through this smoke, menacing but majestic, beastly but beautiful, its breath a force that can take but also give life.

When this dragon appears, you are to take its poison—a medicine that heals but also deals.

Growth does not come without sacrifice.

However, this is a message that goes beyond the need to shed that which no longer serves you!

Shed and sacrifice any and all parts of you

that are no longer needed moving forward. Like a snake shedding its skin, a new you is being formed for your new direction, and your old way of doing things is no longer necessary.

When you are faced with this dragon, be honest with yourself about what is truly called for in your life. Nothing can be hidden from this being who works with such powerful and dark energies.

Medicine does not always taste pleasant going down, but you know the purpose is for long-term healing. We must take responsibility for our actions and deal with the consequences.

4
Hellish Trials

Angel: Malik, Chief of the Angels of
Hell, governs the law of the trials
Element: Fire burns away
self-deception

The gentle yet persistent tapping of the elegant, shiny, ebony claws of a patient, yet smug and devilish, blue being in the shadows reaches your ears. But this dragon waits, biding its time. It knows your weaknesses, it knows your fears, but most of all it knows the path to your downfall.

It whispers from the shadows . . . "Addiction. Indulgence. Temptation." In so doing it highlights what may be your overdependence on and seduction by material and physical pleasures. It's sinfully tantalizing isn't it? . . . Devilish, almost!

When this dragon appears, you are being advised to stop, drop your shoulders, breathe deeply, and take stock of your current situation. Are you living in fear, caged in, or dominated by your own obsessions? Do you harbor an obsession with someone else perhaps? Or is there an area of your life that devours your whole being?

Or are you being deceived? This is a challenging question to answer at the best of times but a poignant and essential one, nonetheless.

Caution is advised! You are on trial and it's up to you to determine who the judge, jury, and executioner are in this courtroom.

Will you pass this devilish test?

The Pride of

THE EARTHLY

5
The Hatching

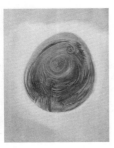

Angel: Gazardiel, Angel of New Beginnings, is guardian to all hatching dragons

Elements: Fire, water, earth, and air—all elements are brought together for new beginnings

The Hatching Dragon's energy emerges from its cosmic egg as ruby-red rays of success, joy, and abundance shine. Can you feel its warmth? The egg is shining on you as it births this new dragon into the world.

There is excitement in the air, chatter amongst the realms, and everyone is asking—What type of dragon will it be?

And yes, you are being asked a similar question here!

When this sparkling little dragon's egg

appears, take it as your clear and certain sign to start something new. A dragon is not told when to hatch, for there is no right or wrong time for its birth. Remember this, because there is also no right or wrong time to start something new.

So what will this new beginning be? The pursuit of a new love, a new chapter in your career, or perhaps something as simple as a project of the heart? Perhaps something even more drastic?

Who cares! Whatever your new adventure may be, know that this newly hatched dragon will be by your side every step of the way.

All you need to do today is accept this sign, start something new, and don't look back in any way.

6
Flame Dancer

Angel: Israfil, Angel of Fire, fuels the
angelic flame of the Fire Dragons
Element: Fire extinguishes obstacles
and lower vibrations

Light a candle and watch its flame dance—this
is your divine connection to the Fire Dragons.

The Fire Dragons are our connection to the
angelic flame; their breath burns away and clears
all obstacles in our path. Fire Dragons will only
work for you if it's for your higher good and will
not interfere with your free will or the free will of
others. Their flame is true and pure of heart. They
are one with fire and nothing can extinguish their
flame.

When the Flame Dancer appears, you are
reminded you can call upon the Fire Dragons to
clear away any and all obstacles in the way of your

success, freedom, and higher purpose in life. Fire Dragons are also useful in clearing lower vibrational thinking and energies around you, your home, and your loved ones. All you need to do is ask for their assistance and they will help.

Take a moment today, light a candle, watch it dance, and breathe deeply three times. When you are ready, call in the Fire Dragons and visualize them coming out of the flame to join you. As they approach, be clear and ask them out loud to burn to the ground any and all obstacles in your way—seen or unseen! Close your eyes and thank the Fire Dragons for their service, then blow out the candle and go about your day.

7

Zephyr's Kiss

Angel: Anpiel, Angel of the Air and Birds, provides direction to the Air Dragons

Element: Air provides clarity of thought and voice

Feel the breeze on your face. It gently lingers then disappears, returning to caress your shoulders and neck. Now it's sitting on your shoulder, gently singing in your ear. That sensation—what is it? Be still. It is a little Air Dragon giving you a kiss with its voice.

The Air Dragons help us connect to the unseen. They teach us to see and to hear by simply feeling our surroundings. As they move with effortless grace through the air, they also clear the energy and raise the vibration of all that is near. Be careful not get too carried away with their infectious vibe though, as we should not always live with our head in the clouds.

When Zephyr's Kiss appears, you are reminded that you can call upon the Air Dragons to clear your energy and raise the vibrations of both yourself and your surroundings. This can be of assistance especially if you're feeling weighed down emotionally and can't feel a way forward. Just ask the Air Dragons to lift your spirits and they will help you feel your way forward in life with grace and ease.

Take a walk outside today. Take three deep breaths and call in the Air Dragons. Feel a slight breeze upon your face, close your eyes, and be still. When you are ready, ask them to clear your energy, raise your vibration, and help usher in refreshing winds to all areas of your life. Once finished, open your eyes and thank them for their service.

8
Earthbound

···············◆···············

Angel: Araquiel, Angel with Dominion
of the Earth, anchors the energy of
the Earth Dragons
Element: Earth grounds your energy

Have you ever noticed how you feel after
spending a day out in nature? Grounded.
Centered. Balanced. There is a presence lingering
around you, keeping you anchored to our Earth. It
is gentle and soothing—it is the work of the Earth
Dragons grounding you to the here and now.

The Earth Dragons assist you in grounding
your energy, balancing your emotions, and filling
you with a sense of calm and tranquility. They are
also called upon following intense spirit or energy
work, which can leave you dizzy, distant, and in
need of anchoring back into the Earth's crystalline energy.

When Earthbound appears, you are reminded that you can call upon the Earth Dragons to assist you in grounding your energy to Earth. Simply visualize them flying gently overhead and spiralling down your body, bringing you back to the present moment, anchored to the Earth's crystalline energy.

Take the time today to place your bare feet on the ground. Close your eyes and wriggle your toes in the dirt, sand, or grass, and call in the Earth Dragons. Feel them gently envelope you in calming, soothing energy, while anchoring you to Earth and grounding you. Stay here as long as you need, then go about your day and thank the Earth Dragons for their service.

9
Drops of Azure

················· ◈ ·················

Angel: Kutiel, Angel of Water and
Divination of Waterways, intensifies
energy generated from the flow of
water

Element: Water assists in cleansing,
flushing, and washing away

There are ripples on a still lake, movement
on its surface, yet nothing is in sight. Waves
crash upon the shore, sweeping back and forth,
yet a single wave breaks against the tide. A river
plods along its course then splits in two, a whirl-
pool dividing its path. This is the dance of the
Water Dragons, their footsteps in the deep.

The Water Dragons assist us with healing on
a physical, energetic, and spiritual level. We are all
born innate healers, and the Water Dragons assist
us in healing by either gently washing away and

clearing our energy or by powerfully flushing out blockages in our body's aura and energy centers.

When Drops of Azure appears, you are reminded that you can call upon the Water Dragons to heal not just yourself, but also others around you, the animals, and the land. Like Fire Dragons, Water Dragons can also clear obstacles in your path. However they are more gentle, tactful, and discreet in nature. This is something to consider and be mindful of when calling in dragons to assist with clearing work.

Take a moment today and immerse yourself in water of any kind: from a shower, a bath, a river, or even the sea. As you do, ask the Water Dragons to wash away all the stagnant energy in your aura and calm your mind. Let them bathe you in their energies. When ready, emerge glowing and clear, and thank the Water Dragons for their service.

10
You, Determined

·············· ◆ ··············

Angel: Tabbris, Angel of Self-
Determination, promotes
self-actualization

Element: Earth and fire assist you in
executing grounded action

Tall and proud, this blue dragon stands with
its golden crest glistening under the bright
sky and its wings held high to help in balance
when traveling. Although this dragon can fly,
it chooses instead to walk the Earth with us, by
our side.

The You, Determined Dragon appears to
implore you to dig deep and have the sheer determined might to be you! Yes, you, the person
you agreed to be before you incarnated on this
amazing Earth.

Remember back to when you were a child.

Who or what did you want to be when you grew up?

Are you that person today?

If not, why not?

This dragon stops and asks you this: Who are you? What are you capable of doing in this life? What have you been putting off for too long because you or someone else talked you out of it?

Close your eyes and see the answer. Once it is firmly in your mind, use this dragon's energy, call upon its strength, forget all your excuses, and just go for it, each and every day!

The You, Determined Dragon speaks to you now, encouraging you to prove to yourself—and only to yourself—that you can be that person your younger self dreamed of being. You can be the best version of you—always, and in all areas of your life!

This dragon is not giving up on you, so neither should you!

11
The Canny Kind

......................◆......................

Angel: Lahash, Angel Who Interferes
with Divine Will, guides this dragon
Element: Earth and air assist in
creating pathways to success

If you look carefully in those rustling leaves, you can just make out the shape of this tiny dragon. It blends in with its surroundings, its beady little eyes darting around, assessing its environment. This dragon might be one of the smallest of them all, but it is cunning and not to be underestimated.

The Canny Kind Dragon emerges when you have to be creative, resourceful, and sometimes squeeze and sneak your way through a situation. Actually, in this regard, it's just like a little critter.

Have you ever noticed how small critters can fit into spaces they know very well they shouldn't be in? But they do so because they are canny, crafty, clever, and they always succeed—almost bending divine will to their advantage.

Well, like those critters, nothing stops this canny dragon—no space is too small, tight, narrow, or dark—and nothing should stop you either!

Almost as if it's an inside secret, this dragon whispers to you to use its energy when you are stuck and brute force simply will not work or has not worked to date. Draw on its cunning wiles to find hidden cracks in the situation, the weaknesses, and maneuver your way through in a flash!

The message this dragon imparts is to be a little selfish in a particular situation in order to ensure a happy outcome for yourself, with minimal fuss and maximum ease.

12
A Steady Wing

Angel: Barrattiel, Angel of Support, stabilizes this dragon's flight

Element: Water and air assist with effortless flow and grace

Is this dragon green or is it blue? Is it smiling or smirking? Is it even a dragon, or is it a phoenix-like bird of prey? As this dragon's energy constantly shifts and evolves, its beautiful feathery body glistens and shimmers in the light. It notices your presence and gets excited, letting out an eagle-like squawk. It then shuffles closer to you. This dragon loves being by your side.

The Steady Wing Dragon appears to teach us about the uncertain times in which we live. Yes, these times *are* tenuous, however, this dragon does not fear that, as tumult always signals that a new era on Earth is near.

From chaos and uncertainty come evolution and growth—always!

This dragon reminds us that uncertain times are the only real certainty. It also reminds us how often we forget those many similar times of old. Our Earth goes in cycles, our soul lives in cycles, and we are simply experiencing a *change* in cycles.

Let it all flow; do not resist. Let it all unfold; do not fear the shifting winds.

The Steady Wing Dragon advises you of the constant truths of our lives: nature is our teacher, the stars are our guides, and we have always weathered uncertain times with the dragons by our side—since the birth of Creation itself, in fact!

Yes, the dragons have and always will be with us in times of upheaval, and now is no exception.

13
A Jovial Breeze

················ ◆ ················

Angel: Tagas, Governing Angel of
  Singing Angels, encourages the
  notes to fall as they may
Element: Air carries the notes and
  uplifts your voice

Just like a tumbler pigeon, this dragon spins and
dances on the unpredictable currents of the air.
It cares not where it lands. It mimics the nature of
a leaf caught in a breeze, handing over control to
the universe. If you listen carefully, really lean in,
you can hear it singing its song: "All Will Fall as
It May . . . " a very fitting idea, given the nature of
this dragon.

This Jovial Breeze Dragon appears to remind
you that like itself, we are often at the mercy of
the ever-shifting universe and its fluxing energies.
Universal timing is no joke. We must learn to go

with the flow of energy, nature, and even the universe itself, to hand over all control and just let go.

We employ a similar concept when we wish to manifest our desires. One mustn't choke the universe. Simply whisper your wishes to the breeze and let this jovial little dragon carry them away.

Take a moment today to stop, breathe deeply, and fall into sync with the breeze. Listen to your thoughts. Are you trying to control too much? Are you fighting constant battles? Feeling stuck? Or just overwhelmed? Honor these thoughts, hand them over to the breeze, and take this dragon's hand—sing, play, and dance with it in the breeze.

All you are being asked to do today is to give over the reins to the universe by listening to a simple song.

14
In Ruins

·········· ◆ ··········

Angel: Pronoia, Ruling Angel Who
Helped Create Mankind, brings
the energy of the ancients to the
forefront of our minds

Element: Earth assists in revealing the
knowledge of the ancients

Still, stoic, and *silent.* These words describe the
In Ruins Dragon, one of the most unusual
dragons you have probably ever seen. It looks like
a combination of many mythical beasts and magical creatures, but it's a dragon nonetheless. There
is an air of sadness to it, for it remembers a time
long ago, a golden age of civilization. This fading
dragon is a reminder of those times and those cultures long past.

They include those of Atlantis and Lemuria,
or even more recently Petra, Troy, Pompeii, and

Angkor Waat. Fallen civilizations all, some vanished, some in ruins, but their wisdom has not been lost, for it resides in this dragon's energy.

The appearance of this dragon indicates that it's time to learn from these ancients. Ask yourself, What can we learn from their fate? Or even, What can we learn from the time before their fall; what can we learn from them during their thriving days? The In Ruins Dragon asks that you honor the memories of these people, their knowledge, and their legacies—and *learn* from their fall. Can we apply those lessons to our current civilization? To a more local degree, can we apply these learnings to our own community?

Can we also apply these learnings to ourselves, right here and now?

Take a moment to reflect on these civilizations, as you never know what you may learn. And in the process, you will keep this beautiful, ancient dragon's energy alive for future generations to come.

15
Silent Muse

···········◆···········

Angel: Dumah, Angel of Silence,
    anchors energy to the here and now
Element: Earth and air create an
    atmosphere of grounded silence

A small, fox-like dragon sits in silence, curled into a ball. It stretches out its vulpine feet every now and again to get comfortable in its resting place, which is nestled in the side of a mountain. It has nowhere to be, and it's happy in the here and now, exuding a calming purple energy to all who are nearby. The small space it occupies is almost like an energy portal radiating this calm energy.

This dragon appears and sees you in your current state of bustling modern-day life.

It simply sits. Watching. Waiting. Wondering. When will you notice its presence? Not that it's getting impatient—again, this dragon has nowhere to be.

The Silent Muse Dragon surfaces when you are in need of silent contemplation. It comes to you now to ask that you gently remove yourself from the conversation with yourself and others.

Find time and a space to be in silence. Contemplate your current situation without an expectation of receiving anything other than silence. Simply be comfortable with yourself in silence, and what is necessary will reveal itself. There is nothing to be forced here.

Do not speak, do not listen, simply muse in silence, for much can be revealed when nothing is said at all.

16
Refracted Reflections

·············· ◆ ··············

Angel: Iaoel, Angel of Visions, enables
clear insight

Element: Air and water give insight
into your life and its direction

Two dragons—no, wait! One dragon? Hard
to say, but they shimmer in the light, a gentle
aqua-green. Their blue aura *refracts* the light, and
their glistening green fur *reflects* the light. This
confuses the eyes. Again, we ask ourselves, is this
one dragon or two?

Regardless, this creature draws near and gently whispers: "It does not matter what we are;
what or who are *you?*"

Is your life a social construct created by the
refracted light of all that is around you? Are you a
victim of circumstance? Or is your life a reflection

of the light within you—a projected vision of how you see yourself?

The Refracted Reflections Dragon appears during times of quandary to remind you that the physical world is never what is seems, nor is it what you wish for it to be, but it is, instead, a sum of all.

You are being told by this dragon to simply stop and do nothing. Take this time out to explore more about who you are at your core by just letting the world around you unfold.

Now is the time for introspective exploration because sometimes the course is not action, but observation.

17

Familia Guardian

Angel: Dubbiel, Guardian Angel of
Persia (also known as a bear god),
protects soul families

Element: Fire and earth create strong
family foundations

Like a big gruff grandfather, this dragon rises
from its rest and lumbers down into our
world. The golden aura surrounding it makes it
appear much larger than it really is. Perhaps this
is a strategy to intimidate and fool the weak of
heart? Indeed—this old dragon is strategic in
many ways.

As it leans in, its intimidating size is negated
by its gentle gaze and it asks, "What is family?"
Hmmm. Good question. Is it your mother, father,
sister, or brother? Is it souls you have incarnated
with over many lifetimes and worlds? Or is it close

friends and people you hold dear in *this* lifetime?

In any event, it doesn't matter; this dragon responds, reminding us that we choose our family!

We choose how to honor them, protect them, and grow with them in this life.

Family is not passive. We should endeavor to create our own unique family made up of many souls. These are people who *complete* our lives; they don't *compete* with us in our lives. Living by these words, you will find your true family!

Do not be fooled by this dragon's gentle, loving nature, for it is also fierce in protecting those who wish to walk away from family—ancestral or otherwise—if the situation warrants that. You do not have to remain in toxic relationships, nor should you expect others to remain in a toxic environment.

18
Gatekeeper

......................◆......................

Angel: Lahabiel, Angel of Protection
(especially against evil spirits),
stabilizes the in-between
Element: Earth, air, water, fire, and
ether combine to create resilient
boundaries

A tall, slender yet powerful dragon stands at
a crossroads, where many gates mark the
passage of the realms. It is silent and radiates an
indigo light to rival that of Archangel Michael
himself. Do not trespass and do not open these
gates without its permission.

This dragon appears when you are neglect-
ing your boundaries. Ah yes! "Boundaries"—an
underrated and often misunderstood concept
on the Earth plane. Boundaries protect our
physical, mental, emotional, and spiritual space,

helping us to maintain our balance and stability in the world.

The presence of this dragon is twofold—you are being reminded to both assess *and* bolster your boundaries. On all levels! Furthermore, you are to remain strong against those who wish to test your boundaries and find it uncomfortable when you do not let them in in the way they desire. The Gatekeeper Dragon acts as the gatekeeper between realms, between heaven and earth, and also between you and the energies of those around you.

It is also often frustrated at just how much disregard we have for such a massively important concept of self! It should also be noted that this dragon only appears when necessary, so please heed its words.

You must ensure that you are the only person holding the keys to the gate that protects your space, place, and self!

The Pride of

THE HEAVENLY

19
Light Source

..................◆..................

Angel: Sabathiel, Angel Who
Communicates Divine Light,
facilitates access to Source via the
blue color spectrum of the sky
Element: Air and ether embody the
blue light of Source communication

Blinding, dazzling blue lights signal this dragon's journey from the heavens. Its stunning, elongated face with piercing eyes portrays an absolute sense of knowing. As it winds its way down to the Earth plane of existence, our energy is drawn up and our vibration is raised so that we and the dragon meet in the middle of heaven and earth—an almost dreamlike state.

This dragon is your introduction to the heavenly divine dragons who reside in the upper planes—the upper angelic realms—and who speak the words of the angels.

When this dragon appears, it heralds a simple but clear message:

> *There is no secret standing in the light;*
> *There is no secret to access Source;*
> *The Light Source is you and always has*
> *been you;*
> *Simply live by this and the Light Source*
> *will be you and always you.*

And that's all that needs to be said.

20
The Indigo

Angel: Diniel, Angel Who Protects
Children, helps (re)awaken an
intuitive, childlike nature
Element: Water and ether embody
the nature of intuition

Familiar and kind, this dragon of crystalline form resides in the mind's eye, a space
between reality and dreams, heaven and earth. Its
smile puts you at ease; you feel it with your soul
instead of seeing it with your eyes. And it has no
voice, simply a presence that speaks. Why is it so
familiar? Have you seen it before . . . perhaps as a
child?

The Indigo Dragon embodies heavenly intuition; that which is not tainted by earthly matters,
and is found in youth but lost in adolescence, and
awoken by the enlightened adult. You may have

heard stories of the Indigo Children, those born with highly intuitive gifts and psychic abilities so innate within their being that they could not imagine life any differently.

When the Indigo Dragon appears, you are being reminded that these children are in fact no different from any other generation—they simply were born knowing who they were from the very beginning.

All you need is a little nudge by this dragon to remember that you also have these gifts. And if you are one of those enlightened adults, you are to remember to keep honing and working with these gifts; do not become complacent.

Flowing from its crystal-like crown of horns, let the Indigo Dragon flood your aura with the indigo spectrum of light and (re)awaken your intuition, strengthening your connection to the Divine.

21
Healer's Calling

Angel: Suriel, Angel of Healing, holds
  space for healing and allows its flow
Element: Air and ether embody the
  healing capacities of angelic breath

With a ruffle of its feathery mane, healing green energy falls upon all in its presence. The Healer's Calling Dragon is a horned, bird-like dragon with the body of a Pegasus. It is graceful and curious and exudes heavenly healing with its every movement and angelic breath.

The presence of this dragon is in response to a calling within your soul; a call to arms by the heavens to remember your soul's purpose. Yes, you are being commanded by the Divine to heal, and to be the healer in all forms of the word.

The Healer's Calling Dragon advises that, should you already be a healer in this lifetime, you are to undertake this role with grace and dignity, guided by its heavenly presence. Call it in when healing yourself, others, or even the Earth. Let it hold space for you from the heavens above.

A healer's calling need not be the quintessential, traditional path or career in medicine or even spiritual healing. For this dragon reminds us that a healer walks many paths in many lifetimes. One can heal in the most unconventional manner and way. All you need do is surrender to your role, to your calling, and the healing energy will flow where needed, guided by this beautiful heavenly dragon.

22
Heart Truth

Angel: Miniel, Angel Invoked to Induce
Love, assists this dragon to ride the
lightning bolts of heavenly love

Element: Fire and ether assist you in
passionately embodying divine truth

A scarlet mist appears, a wall of luscious red energy forms, and a flash of lightning from the heavens heralds this fierce dragon. It stands tall, with wings that reach back up to the skies from which it descended, glistening in the residual energy of the heavenly lightning bolts. It settles, shakes off its slumber, and turns to you, reaching out with its almost feline-like paw to point to your heart.

The heart is often a symbol of love. Indeed, it pumps passionate red energy though our bodies. Every beat puts us a step closer to our earthy, lustful desire and it skips a beat when our true love is near!

However this dragon appears to say that this is not the case for our soul, as the heart is the driver of our truth. The heart is the engine room for what truly drives us on a spiritual level, and aligns us to our higher purpose in life and on our soul's journey through many lives.

This dragon leans in and places its forehead to yours—a dragon's kiss, the sign of dragon love. It is infusing your soul, your being, with the courage to speak your heart's truth.

Place your hand on your heart and do not focus on what words will be spoken by this truth. Simply hold this dragon's energy in your heart, visualizing the dragon's kiss—and the truth will flow.

Smile, give this dragon a kiss back, and you will always speak your heart's truth, the words of the Divine!

23
Magic in Reality

················ ◆ ················

Angel: Nuriel, Angel of Spellbinding,
   is the source of this dragon's magic
Element: Ether and air embody a
   child's wish sent to heaven

From the mists of Avalon, a place lost in time somewhere in the heavenly realms of the angels, comes this dragon. It slides down the currents of wishes sent from the children of Earth just like a water serpent rides the currents of a stream. As it moves, this secretive dragon, with an almost lurid green body, leaves no trace—it does not wish to be found or followed.

This creature is the guardian of celestial magic, the alchemy of the heavens, where reality and wonder create all that is impossible—and all that is possible pales in comparison. Once experienced, your world will never be the same again.

This dragon rarely appears, for who would want to leave Avalon so freely? However when it does it is so much more than just a call to remember and to believe in magic again.

It is a blatant call, straight from the celestial beast's mouth, to *create* magic! This dragon is your teacher, your guide. His story in your life is a tale more enchanting than that of the proverbial sorcerer and his apprentice.

Your first step on this magical quest is to close your eyes, visualize your favorite natural landscape from childhood, and meet this dragon there. See it tumbling down from the sky to meet you in this magical place. Sit with it and play with it, and in so doing, learn the language of a child's wish once more.

Visit this place any time you wish to create magic. Call in this lustrous green dragon to bless your visions, and from the heavens will come your creations, guided by the magic of Avalon!

24
Soul of Soleil

························ ◆ ························

Angel: Sorath, Angel Who Is the Spirit
of the Sun, is the source of healing
warmth and light

Element: Ether and fire embody
celestial fire

The warmth of this dragon glows from within and cleanses your soul instantly when it's near. Incandescent radiant light streams from its body so brightly that it appears translucent. Its head is adorned with searingly hot horns and surrounded by an aura of searing white heat. This dragon does not need wings, for its celestial fire propels it across our Earth like the solar flares of its birthplace, the sun.

Our sun is a celestial being with brothers and sisters in the millions. He is the giver of life, the center of our universe, a star like any other.

However, this fiery celestial caregiver is our star, and his soul is this dragon gifted to the Earth just for us.

You are being reminded by this dragon to harness the power of the sun to cleanse your energetic field and clear the way for a stronger connection to the Divine. This is a simple but effective action one can take for one's personal development, emotional care, and spiritual growth. Many cultures around the world use sun gazing for well-being and spiritual enhancement. Modern-day science also appreciates the valuable vitamin D, which our body can only create by being in the presence of the sun.

Simply stand in the sun's presence, call in the Soul of Soleil Dragon, and let the golden rays of sunshine pour over you like liquid gold. As you are cleansed, your inner glow begins to shine just as brightly as this dragon until you and it are one—combining to become a single solar flare shooting outward for all the world's benefit.

Send this celestial fire to the world, and watch it inspire!

25
Iridium Moon

Angel: Asariel, Angel Who Rules the
Moon, is called upon to help you
achieve your goals

Element: Ether and water embody
ever-flowing, transformational
energy

The sapphire blue eyes of this dragon are seen in the stormiest of nights as it looks lovingly upon the Earth. Its golden-quartz, crystal-like body is sleek and it floats across the night sky with effortless ease and grace. This dragon needs not exert its energy to outshine the sun, as it has the power to absorb and transmute solar energy just like the landscape of its birthplace, the moon.

Our moon is a living being and a celestial goddess with rays of light more piercing than the sun but gentler on the soul. Her many phases and their many applications in our world are well documented throughout ancient mythical traditions. Rituals, harvests, magic energies, and coastal tides ebb and flow with her cyclic movements and the lunar patterns in the sky.

You are being taught by this dragon that you can harness the powers of the moon to do so much more than manifest or clear that which does not serve; it also activates a divine secret within us.

This secret is that we can call upon any phase of the moon, and its respective utility, at any given time.

Your intention is the key that unlocks these divine transformational energies, no matter the phase, cycle, or time.

"How?" you might ask.

"It's simple!" this dragon responds with a wink of its sapphire eyes. "Focus on what you wish to achieve and then ask the moon to assist." Switch from thinking you must follow a cycle and instead create your own timeline. It is all about intent, and your divine desire to create!

26
Heavenly Whispers

········· ◆ ·········

Angel: Hermesiel, Angel of the
Heavenly Choirs, unifies the many
angelic voices in the choirs of
heaven

Element: Ether and air embody the
heavenly voices

There is a blue shimmer in the clouds, and a distant melody is heard as this mystical, fox-like dragon shimmies across the skies. This dragon hums along to the songs of the angels. It closes its eyes and trusts where the music will take it, for it knows that the heavenly choir divinely guides the way.

The choirs of heaven sing their songs and on their voices this dragon rides. This dragon is the niggle, the nudge—that nagging twinge in your intuition that you just should not ignore.

Slow your mind, place your hands on your ears, and tune into your inner ear to listen to this dragon's whisper. It sings to turn left, go right, stop and pause, to go forth with zeal and passion. This dragon is guiding you at every step with every lyric, every beat. Join in with it, scream and shout with your own heavenly voice, and sing a song for no reason at all other than to join in with the choir of heaven. Singing with this dragon in this way will ensure that every necessary lyric, beat, and melody is heard. Don't fear that you will not hear these heavenly whispers, for the dragons understand that at times it may be difficult for us humans to tune into the celestial calls.

Trust this gentle little dragon—ask out loud to hear its music and it will share the heavenly songs with you every moment of your day.

27
Angelic Wisdom

·············· ◆ ··············

Angel: Barman, Angel of Intelligence, is
mentor to the angels and this dragon
Element: Ether and water embody
the flow of angelic wisdom

A most traditional-looking dragon sits
patiently on the edge of a mountain, high
up in the sky. There are no birds up here, no white
noise, just the misty clouds shrouding its place of
rest. This dragon exudes the confidence we all
seek. It knows what it knows, and is in no rush to
prove this to any man, beast, or being.

It is gifted with a divine knowing . . . a
trusting . . . it leans into the wisdom of the heavens without hesitation, and fully surrenders.

When this dragon of Angelic Wisdom
appears, invite it to sit patiently by your side while
you too lean into the wisdom of the heavens and

are imbued with the knowledge of the angelic realms.

Close your eyes, see this vibrant red dragon with golden eyes in your mind's eye, and just trust it to hold your space as you open your heart to the wisdom that's about to unfold. Place your hand on your heart and draw your attention to this space. See it opening more and more each day. Journal every thought, image, and word that comes to you when you sit with this dragon, and accept its guidance with an open heart and mind.

This dragon will never lead you astray, so simply surrender to its angelic knowledge and trust it, which is all it asks you to do.

28
Dreams I Dream

·············· ◆ ··············

Angel: Duma, Angelic Prince of
Dreams, walks side by side with this
dragon in the astral plane
Element: Ether embodies the pure
energy of astral dreams

Suspended in motion, drifting between time,
space, reality, and dreams, this tiny magenta
dragon smiles while it sleeps, and chirps little pink bubbles of light as it snores away. This
dragon gently drifts in and out of sleep, cooing as
it watches your dreams float by; it is content and
blessed in its existence in the Dream State.

The Dream State is where worlds, realms,
and the unseen meet in the astral plane. Some say
that one who accesses this state masters the ability
to bring dreams into reality and creates a literal
heaven on Earth.

When this dragon appears, it's asking you to close your eyes, invite it close, and take a long, restful sleep before traveling to the astral plane. Don't worry how you'll get there, simply find a safe, comfortable place and allow yourself to drift off with this dragon by your side.

Here in the Dream State, or the astral plane, you will find the answers you seek. Here your earthly mind walks in the mists of the heavens and inspiration strikes like magenta lightning bolts, guided by this dragon as it flies above you.

Upon waking from this heavenly slumber, it doesn't matter if you remember the visions provided to you in this state. This dragon does, and it will remind you exactly when needed.

29
Heavenly Fortunate

Angel: Sachiel, Angel of Wealth, Success, and Prosperity, guides this dragon

Element: Ether, water, and fire embody the flow of golden abundance

A rainbow dragon of ancient Chinese mythology dances across the sky. Ringing bells of all kinds herald its presence, and the sound of golden coins lingers in the ear. With a serpent-like body, consisting of the brightest, most vibrant colors, this dragon spreads abundance and joy straight from the heavens.

The vibrant, joyful Heavenly Fortunate Dragon's role is to teach us to manifest abundance, success, and prosperity from a place of freedom. As they fly above us in the heavens, they advise us to not focus on monetary wealth or to try to manipulate the universe for loose change.

Instead, manifest freedom, from which all aspects of abundance flow. Freedom is the currency of the dragons!

Take a moment now to think about what freedom means to you. What does it look, feel, sound, and smell like? Yes, use all your senses to make the feeling of freedom as real and tangible as possible. Once you have a clear and incredibly detailed vision about what freedom means to you, thank the Heavenly Fortunate Dragon for making this reality exist. Be present and in the moment, and thank this dragon as if it's already happening! Thank it for this freedom.

Remember, you will always be abundant and have an auspicious life when you are free to walk the path of light, free to love, and free to follow your higher purpose in life.

30
Serendipitous

························◆························

Angel: Kabshiel, Angel of Grace and
Favor, ensures that chance is in your
favor

Element: Ether and air embody the
intangible nature of serendipity

This heavenly beast resembles a unicorn but is
a dragon nonetheless, with two unicorn-like
horns lining its forehead and the sweet face of a
pony. Timid and shy, it shuffles back and forth
as it interacts with other celestial beasts such as
unicorns and other dragons. It recognizes both as
kin, and straddles the fine line between the two
races of mythical beings.

This unusual Serendipitous Dragon comes
from a place within a glimmer of a moment cap-
tured in a single pulse of light. It is the embodiment of serendipity, those moments we often

confuse for coincidental chance and just push aside. This dragon sees all possibilities flowing from a single, chance moment, and aligns us perfectly to the most advantageous outcome for our higher purpose.

This dragon appears to remind us that moments of alignment are not something we can force or foresee. They are fleeting, yet their effects are felt across the realms and one must not struggle against the tide of destiny.

Place your trust in this all-seeing dragon to guide you through serendipity and through moments of life that are momentary and swift but hold tremendous purpose and heavenly guidance.

The next time serendipity shows up in your life, seize the moment and be grateful for the opportunities this dragon arranges for you from the heavens above.

31
Eternity Eternal

············· ◆ ·············

Angel: Lamechial, Angel Who Thwarts
Deception, empowers this dragon
to shatter the misconception of time

Element: Ether and water embody
the continuous flow of eternity

A long black serpent dragon with piercing red
eyes roars though the midnight sky like a
shooting star. Its body bends, twists, and forms
the infinity symbol as it travels down from the
heavens. It is the embodiment of infinite eternity
and knows no reason, just like time itself.

This dragon appears to teach us the simplicity of eternity and the underlying comfort it can
provide us during the darkest of days. With the
knowledge that time is eternal and our days constantly change, we are provided with reassurance
by this dragon, for it teaches us that our current

situation will always come to an end and a new dawn will arise.

Eternity provides hope through constant change!

This dragon also thwarts the deceptions of those around us who seek to keep us in a holding pattern that posits that all is bleak in our world. Let the Eternity Eternal Dragon raise your vibration and break free of this illusion.

This dragon has witnessed countless times in human history where all have felt lost and the sun had set on times of abundance and joy. However these times were not permanent, and the sun rose again, ushered in by this fierce, determined dragon of Eternity Eternal.

32
Among the Stars

Angel: Kokabel, Prince Angel of the
Stars, gifted this dragon to the
universe
Element: Ether embodies cosmic life-
force energy

Sirius, Pleiades, or Arcturus—simple star constellations or galactic civilizations in the stars?

This galactic dragon is made up of the combined consciousnesses of these star races, created
by the explosive death of a star many, many eons
ago. Neon, cosmic, constantly shifting colors create the illusion of a dragon, but they are more
spirit than beast; more ether than energy.

A star seed is a soul who has lived many, if
not most, of their incarnated lives as a galactic
being among the stars. Are you a star seed? Can
you hear the call of the stars and your distant soul

family who inhabit the constellations above this Earth?

This is not a deafening, colliding sound, nor it is a blinding, supernova light.

It is a silent yearning for a home you never knew existed but wished was near.

Let this galactic dragon take you there in spirit. Close your eyes and ride its cosmic waves past the heavens and into the galaxies far beyond the reaches of what can be imagined. Ask this dragon to send out a call to your cosmic soul family so they can meet you in your dreams.

Let this dragon always ensure that you have stardust on your feet and the cosmos in your heart!

The Pride of

THE ARCHANGELS

33
Celestial Mosaics

········· ◆ ·········

Archangel: Archangel Jophiel is
adorned in scarlet robes and holds
the divine scepter of truth

The first of the Archangel Dragons, who are
ethereal and somewhat surreal beasts, is this
phoenix-like dragon with luscious, scarlet-red
wings and a vibrant blue-green body; a sight to
behold. Wise, knowing, and proud, it steps forward to you and passes on Archangel Jophiel's
message:

> *Divine wisdom and understanding is*
> *innate within you;*
> *A birthright decreed by celestial beings*
> *who predate even the dragons and*
> *the angels themselves.*

This dragon soars above the heavens from Seraphim, the celestial home of the angels, showering you in the light of the Celestial Mosaics, a divine kaleidoscopic energy accessible to all.

The presence of Jophiel's dragon heralds a new era in which you realize this truth, where you finally understand—you are a channel of the Divine!

There is no secret, there is no hidden key to this ability, for your very existence is divinely blessed, and from this truth comes the realization that yes, you too are divine.

Bathe in the light of Jophiel's Dragon; bathe in its rainbow colors. Celebrate your newfound truth, and bring forward the Divine to humanity.

Be the channel.

34
Gaian Star

············· ❖ ·············

Archangel: Archangel Ariel has ruby
wings and wears an emerald crown

Amost petite, pretty little green dragon of the
archangels watches you in silence. It waits
patiently for your breathing to be in sync with
the heartbeat of Gaia—our earthly yet celestial
home, this dragon's mother and guide. One might
mistake this dragon for a more earthly, nature
sprite-like being. However the ruby crown float-
ing above its elegant head gives away its Seraphim
nature.

Ariel's dragon is the celestial guardian of
flora and fauna on Earth, a fierce protector who,
despite its size, will strike with archangel-like
power and precision when pushed. This dragon
appears rarely, but when it does, it sings to you the
stories of the stars, who are the sisters of Gaia:

When the stars shine their light, it is
seen for distances beyond even their
comprehension.
A star's warmth sustains life across the
universe, yet it asks for nothing in
return.
When a star dies, its pain is felt by the
remaining stars, each of whom take
in the energy of their fallen sibling
and shine more brightly in its name.
Children of Earth, your Gaian mother
implores you to always be guided by
the wisdom of the stars.
And to remember that your souls are as
powerful as the stars.

Remember the stories of the stars as told by Ariel's Dragon. Follow its lead and shine in your own way, strong and true!

35
Sacred Warrior

························◆························

Archangel: Archangel Haneal is
accompanied by his purple shield,
engraved with a sacred heart

A warm, gentle, familiar purple face fills your mind's eye. It features golden eyes and an aura as bright as neon aquamarine. Who is this loving beast who seems so familiar? You feel as though you know it from somewhere. The fact is, you *do*. For it's Archangel Hanael's sacred dragon who has been calling you, since your birth, to take up arms as a Sacred Warrior.

Do not be fearful of this call—you are ready and have been ready for a long time now. Lean into the image of this dragon in your mind's eye and ask it for guidance. When it arrives, trust the guidance you've so generously received.

In return, Hanael's dragon surrounds you

with Divine Masculine energy, and asks you to close your eyes and to focus on your breath and your heartbeat—all of which are your keys to the Divine.

Notice that it is in your nature to simply breathe without thought and also to love from your heart without thought; these instinctive acts are simple keys to connecting with the Divine every day.

Connecting with the Divine every day is an innate ability in each and every one of us! It is the simple act of breathing along with the simple act of loving; the simple act of *being*. You are being asked to accept this and let the knowledge, wisdom, and love of the Divine flow through you more and more each day.

Trust this, know this, and understand that you are a Sacred Warrior of the Divine, being called to connect the breath to the heart and take action today!

36
Godly Foundations

Archangel: Archangel Sandalphon wears a crown of angelic fire and navy blue robes

An intimidating, powerful dragon with a mane of fiery feathers and midnight-blue wings as long as the night sky rules the lower realms of Seraphim. A truly magnificent dragon, as tall and as grand as its archangel guardian, Archangel Sandalphon, who is known as being exceedingly tall among the angels of the Seraphim.

Traveling on angelic fire across the realms, it booms across the universe, shaking the cosmic dust off our sleepy souls and proclaiming, "Your foundation is you!"

Can you hear its words? Sandalphon's powerful dragon is reminding you that:

Your foundation is you;
Ever present but you're never aware;
Why place your foundations in that of
    another, that whichever changes,
    ever sways;
Anchor your light to yourself and see it
    transform into an ever-present and
    ever-aware godly foundation that is
    simply you.

Like the dragons, angels, and unicorns, you are a gift from the celestials, the gods themselves.

Allow this knowledge to stabilize your godly foundation.

37
Righteously, You

Archangel: Archangel Zadkiel is clad in purple robes and holds a thunderbolt high in the sky

Electric blue lightning strikes across the realms, as a sparkling, griffin-like dragon charges these bolts of angelic energy and discharges them upon each breath. This is no fire-breathing dragon of old. No, it lives in the storm clouds of Seraphim and is proud to be different. It righteously takes on its role as being divinely unique and different from all other dragons, proud to stand out among the prides.

Archangel Zadkiel's dragon appears out of nowhere, with no warning or sign, to remind you, during times when the darkness creeps in, to know this:

You are the sum of all—earth, air, fire,
water, and ether combined. You are
made up of the light and the dark,
and every gradient in between,
You will always be a unique combination
of all elements,
You are not just the light; you are not just
the dark,
You will never be like anyone else,
It is in the in-between moments of life
Where your soul has its human
experience.

Acknowledge this wisdom granted to you by Zadkiel's dragon. The ups, downs, and sometimes sideways moments of life—these are the divinely gifted human experiences wherein you grow, learn, and move closer to your true nature and higher self.

Understand this and know that you are destined to be you, righteously you, and no one else!

38
Celestial Love

···········◆·············

Archangel: Archangel Chamuel wears
purple robes and holds the keys to
the Garden of Eden

The original Garden of Eden, nestled in the Indus Valley, is surrounded by cliffs higher than human comprehension and is held in secret by the angels of Seraphim. It is in this place that the most beautiful of all the Archangel Dragons resides. Its long, sleek, opulent white body slinks its way around the cliffs up high and its pure white, opal-like eyes gaze lovingly into the garden below.

This is Archangel Chamuel's dragon, the literal jewel in the crown of the archangel's pride. It's a most pure dragon whose simple role is to spread celestial love across the realms.

Chamuel's dragon appears to those who give

their love too willingly in the service of others,
and is here to remind them of this:

> *Children of Earth, remember you cannot*
>   *love them all;*
> *You are not here to love, to guide, and*
>   *to steer all on their higher path.*
>   *Nor are you here to love all to your*
>   *detriment.*
> *Inspire, lead, and teach where you can,*
>   *when you can, and how you can, but*
>   *leave the rest up to them.*
> *Just because the world needs you to spread*
>   *love now more than ever doesn't*
>   *mean that you do not deserve love in*
>   *return.*
> *Your soul requires just as much love as*
>   *everyone else's.*

Hold tightly onto these words when you feel
like you have given too much to the world.

39

Serene Is the Night

·············· ◆ ··············

Archangel: Archangel Jerahmiel is in white robes and holds the Evening Star

Serene, calm, and tranquil energy emanates from this white Archangel Dragon as it shimmers between the realms of the Seraphim and Earth. It travels on the prayers, spells, and blessings of those who lie awake at night, weary and overtired from feeling the love, the pain, and everything else in between of others. This is otherwise known as the Night of the Awake.

Archangel Jerahmiel's dragon appears to those very few sensitive souls who know too well the Night of the Awake and tells you this:

*For those of you who are more sensitive
than the rest, the ones who see, who
feel, and who love so deeply,*

*The ones who lie awake at night and
yearn for their home among the
realms of the angels,*

*Those of whom yearn to feel normal and
to know where they fit in with this
world, remember this: your soul
chose this path, for it knew you were
strong enough.*

*It is in those moments when you are
awake at night, feeling everything—
vulnerable and anxious—that the
angels, the dragons, and the Divine
are closer to you than ever.*

*Reach out to them and feel their presence
in the silent serenity of the night, for
that is when we are able to hear the
Divine so clearly.*

40
Cosmic Healing

Archangel: Archangel Raphael is in
rainbow robes and holds a staff of
Asclepius

Green is the color of a healer's aura, or so they say! In the realms of the Seraphim, healing takes on all colors of the spectrum, and so too does this dragon take on another image, not tied down to the confines of tradition.

Golden is this eagle-like dragon of Raphael, with feathers of purple and aquamarine with a slight tinge of gold; its presence is so dazzling it blinds the most powerful of angels.

Archangel Raphael's dragon appears to remind you of this simple celestial truth—your breath heals.

This world of ours goes through an ever-evolving state of change, flux, and turmoil.

However, the one constant is your ability to heal yourself and others through your breath, on a cosmic level.

There is no secret to this ability, nor a key to unlocking its potential. All you need do is stop, breathe deeply, and take in the energy of Raphael's dragon, its purple, gold, and aquamarine aura filling your soul.

Overflowing from your heart, this dragon's energy surrounds you in a pool of cosmic healing and creates a beautiful bubble that suspends you in an energetic space between the realms. Stay here for as long as you need, resting in the light of Raphael's dragon, and send out healing to yourself, others, and the cosmos simply by breathing.

Know and trust that you can come back to this space whenever healing is needed on any level.

41
Divine Lore

.... ◆ ....

Archangel: Archangel Metatron is in golden robes and holds a silver Merkaba

Silvery grey is this dragon, reminiscent of the fairy tales of the magic British Isles of old—but it's a Seraphim Dragon nonetheless. This is a truly intimidating, grand dragon of the archangels. It has hawk-like wings and the body of a lion, with the horns of a ram on its head, crowning its crystal-blue eyes that see all there is to see across the realms.

Archangel Metatron's dragon, guardian of his lore—the celestial intelligence of the Seraphim—stands proudly among the great hall of the archangels, a place where all wisdom, logic, magic, and science is kept in situ for eternity.

From all the knowledge and wisdom contained in Metatron's lore, Metaron's dragon steps forward to you now to simply say this:

> *Learn from your own mistakes, not those*
> *of others.*
> *Perception, perspective, and people are all*
> *diverse, different, and dangerous to*
> *compare—especially to yourself!*
> *Learn from yourself, and yourself only!*
> *Expect more of yourself. And only yourself!*

One might be mistaken and dismiss this message due to its simplicity, but when it is practiced this dragon will unlock the more complex lore of Metatron for you.

42
Infinite Embodiment

Archangel: Archangel Gabriel holds a
white sword of angelic light

Thousands of voices sing and rejoice in the name of the Seraphim. "Rejoice!" these one thousand pure white dragons sing as they fly through the realms via a portal of purples and blues—the colors of the Divine Feminine. These are the dragons of Gabriel, her heralds, her choir, and her steeds of pure Seraphim light.

Hear their voices call out to you; over and over they sing Gabriel's words. Place your hands on your heart to hear their song. Your heart, the divine gateway to the angels, is where Gabriel's dragons are guiding you to go: inside yourself and through to the Portal of Veer.

Veer is a portal of the Seraphim where we can

access angelic energies to love, heal, and reform absolutely anything in our lives—past, present, or future. Here we encounter birth, death, and a rebirth of the consciousness to worlds beyond our own. Take your time and do not rush on this newfound journey through Veer that's being presented to you now.

No one can tell you what lies at the end of this journey or what wonderment awaits you along the way. This is your time—a time when your inner guidance is being sought to navigate this newfound path, and you must take your time to explore, experiment, and experience all its wonders.

What is being shown to you here is the Portal of Veer—the infinite embodiment of the infinite power of Archangel Gabriel's gathering of dragons and their transformational magic.

43

Temple of Light

Archangel: Archangel Uriel holds a
torch lit with the Christ Light flame

The embodiment of Christ Light itself,
this dragon has no form, shape, or body. It
appears simply as the collective flames of the
Seraphim, too bright for us mere humans to gaze
upon without Archangel Uriel filtering out its
blinding rays.

Uriel's dragon appears to remind us that our
light often shines more powerfully inside us like
an oil-lit flame in a hidden temple lost long ago,
rather than outward, fueled by ego and lust. It is a
single oil-lit flame holding its power within a vast,
cavernous, sacred citadel of the ancients.

Through his dragon, Archangel Uriel, an
ambassador of the light, is advising you of this:

*Your divine light does not always shine
    outward; nor does it need to do so.*
*Do not wish to shine your divine light
    for all the world to see and do not
    always seek to shine so that others
    can see.*
*Perhaps, just perhaps, let them seek out
    your light.*
*Let them find that hidden temple, which
    is actually a vast glistening city
    reserved for the very few.*

These are divinely lit words to live by at any time.

44
Sword of Deliverance

·············· ⬧ ··············

Archangel: Archangel Michael holds a
sword burning with Christ Light flames

An archangel's sword is the most powerful of
weapons in the Seraphim's armory and the
same applies to this dragon. Here we meet a giant,
bronze-red, Nordic-like dragon, ripped from the
terrifying tales of the Vikings. It has huge horns,
Michael's blue aura, and a fiery gaze that stares
through the realms.

This dragon's size is immeasurable by human
standards and its sheer power unstoppable. It is
capable of destroying whole mountains, lands,
and worlds with a single fiery breath. Truly a
dragon of Archangel Michael, this is the most
powerful celestial beast of all the prides and absolutely knows no fear.

Michael's dragon leads the march of his Army of Light, an armada advancing across the realms in the name of the Christ Light itself.

This dragon recites Michael's war cry across the realms and bellows:

I am the light. I fight for you in the light. I
protect you with the light. I stand with you
in the light.
Can you hear that sound, just to the right? It
is my dragon; my sword of angelic fire,
crackling and sparkling. It's ready for
anyone who may challenge you in the light!
You are the leader of your own battalion, so call
upon my dragon and with him march as
one unified body of light across your Earth.
United as one, never divided, united as one,
never defeated!

You are being called to soldier forward, so take up the Sword of Deliverance and fight with the Army of Light.

About the Author

Angelo Thomas is a natural-born spirit medium and earth-angel incarnate who spreads his celestial wings far and wide to function as a bridge between humanity and spiritual beings in all forms. Angelo works daily with spiritual beings from the angelic realms (archangels, dragons, and unicorns), as well as the ascended masters, galactic star beings, and even the Fae.

Since he was sixteen, Angelo has been bringing forward messages of guidance, healing, and love from spirits and the angelic realms for people from all walks of life. From his humble beginnings on the streets of the Greek Islands, reading the tarot in his teens, Angelo now provides readings, healings, and spiritual development coaching internationally. He also facilitates Platform Mediumship events and spiritual development workshops across Australia.

Angelo's mission is to inspire everyone to

access the Divine every day, teach people to receive guidance and healing from their spirit team, and activate the light codes within everyone, enabling them to remember who they truly are in this lifetime.

It was Angelo's personal dragon guide, Rían, the Pendragon of the Pride of Dragons deck, a powerfully ancient angelic beast, who inspired him to create this project. Rían has been with Angelo since he was young, and was the inspiration for his lifelong obsession with the Realm of the Dragons.

Angelo has presented numerous workshops on the dragons and their role in our spiritual development and the ascension process and continues to spread their wisdom throughout the world. More information on his spiritual work can be found at **www.AngeloThomas.au**.

About the Artist

Sonja Hedger discovered a love of painting in 2017—and hasn't put her brush down since! With a background in spiritual consulting, energy modalities, and coaching, Sonja wanted to share simple messages in an engaging and creative way. This drive became the inspiration for her business endeavor, Iridium Soul. Sonja's first deck of oracle cards in 2019—The Elementools—was the beginning of a new path for her.

Sonja has known Angelo Thomas for several years and has loved working with him to produce the enlightening Pride of Dragons deck. The Realm of the Dragons first introduced themselves to her during a session with a client wherein she was introduced to her new guide Louie. He is a very mischievous dragon who arrived to help Sonja navigate her next spiritual adventure.

Sonja and Angelo share a passion for putting their divine messages and information into beautiful oracle cards for all to share and learn from. With the help and guidance of Angelo's teachings, Sonja worked with these majestic beings to bring her experience and knowledge into this earthly realm and into the hands and hearts of all who will enjoy and benefit from working with this deck.

More information on Sonja's work can be found at **Facebook.com/iridiumsoul**.

Books of Related Interest

Dragon Wisdom
43-Card Oracle Deck and Book
by Christine Arana Fader • illustrated by Anja Kostka

Soul Helper Oracle
Messages from Your Higher Self
by Christine Arana Fader • illustrated by Elena Dudina

Soulflower Plant Spirit Oracle
44-Card Deck and Guidebook
by Lisa Estabrook

Chakra Cards for Belief Change
The Healing InSight Method
by Nikki Gresham-Record

Empath Activation Cards
Discover Your Cosmic Purpose
by Rev. Stephanie Red Feather, Ph.D.

The Female Archangels Oracle
A 44-Card Empowerment Deck and Guidebook
by Calista • illustrated by Marie-Joe Fourzali

Celtic Healing Oracle
64 Cards and Guidebook
by Rosemarie Anderson, Ph.D. • illustrated by Susan Dorf

INNER TRADITIONS • BEAR & COMPANY
P.O. Box 388
Rochester, VT 05767
1-800-246-8648 • www.InnerTraditions.com